DARTMOUTH LYRICS

DARTMOUTH LYRICS

BY

RICHARD HOVEY

EDITED BY

EDWIN OSGOOD GROVER

BOSTON
SMALL, MAYNARD & COMPANY
PUBLISHERS

Printed in the United States of America

THE MURRAY PRINTING COMPANY
THE BOSTON BOOKBINDING COMPANY
CAMBRIDGE, MASS.

TO
MEN OF DARTMOUTH

THE FOREWORD

RICHARD HOVEY was Dartmouth's Laureate — the great interpreter of the Dartmouth Spirit. He revealed us to ourselves.

Nowhere else is the spirit and personality of the College so faithfully and so stirringly expressed as in his poem, "Men of Dartmouth." Here in three stanzas he crystallized the spiritual ideals of which the College was born, and which have given it those qualities of loyalty, comradeship, and sturdy manhood that have created for it a distinct personality among American colleges.

A surprising number of Hovey's poems are associated with Dartmouth College either directly or indirectly. The purpose of the present volume is to gather together, primarily for Dartmouth men, those of his poems that relate to the College and to college life. The volume includes the best* of the poems he contributed to the college publications during his undergraduate life, the poems contributed after graduation, the poems read at various Dartmouth banquets, the songs written for the first edition of "Dartmouth Songs" together with a number of older lyrics that were given musical settings for this volume. Also the "Dartmouth Ode" read at the one hundred twenty-fifth anniversary of the College, and the rollicking poems read by him at the several conventions of

* Hovey's literary activity while at Dartmouth is evidenced by the fact that in addition to the undergraduate poems in this volume he contributed thirty additional poems to the college publications. None of them, however, seems worthy to be included here.

the Psi Upsilon Fraternity. This group of lyrics of college life forms a definite and stimulating contribution to the literature of Dartmouth.

The purpose of this volume is to help carry on the sturdy qualities of the Dartmouth Spirit, and tie up Richard Hovey's name more closely as "Dartmouth's Laureate."

THE CONTENTS

RICHARD HOVEY

In the larger literary sense Richard Hovey belongs to America to whose permanent literature he made a substantial and worth-while contribution. When you recall that he died at thirty-five, just as he was coming into the fullness of his poetic powers, with an assured income and leisure for writing, it is impossible to overestimate what he might have accomplished if he had been given another thirty-five years for productive work. What he did accomplish, however, reconciles us, for his work runs to a dozen volumes and bears the mark of high literary art and passionate love of living.

In another and real sense Richard Hovey belonged to Dartmouth College. He came to Hanover a seventeen-year-old boy from the Washington, D. C., high school. He left, a man of twenty-one with his mind enriched, his literary ambitions stimulated and a new sense of the joy and meaning of life.

From the first he took himself and his literary work seriously and dedicated himself to his task with a devotion that must have yielded a full harvest if the Reaper had not appeared so soon.

While at College Richard Hovey lived a busy and profitable life. He was an editor of *The Dartmouth* during his freshman, sophomore, and junior years and managing editor of *The Aegis* his junior year. He wrote the sophomore class history under the title, "Hanover by Gas Light, or Ways That Are Dark." He won the prize for dramatic speaking in both his junior and senior years and upon graduation won the Phi Beta Kappa key. He also took final honors *cum laude* in English language and literature. He was equally active in the social life of the College as well as in the Psi Upsilon Fraternity of which he was a member.

Out of these four years of creative living Richard Hovey developed a love and loyalty for Dartmouth that never left him. He came from the artificial life of Washington into the simplicity of college life as it then existed at Dartmouth. He found the comradeship of strong men, the inspiration of great teachers, notably Prof. C. F. Richardson. He gloried in the outdoor life of the College and no man ever left Hanover with a keener sense of the brooding message of the "still North," the "hill winds," the "granite of New Hampshire" and the winter days when " the great white cold walks abroad."

The writer will never forget the impression of majesty and sincerity which pervaded the poem entitled, "Comrades," which Hovey read in the old gymnasium on the occasion of the sixtieth anniversary of the Psi Upsilon Convention, May 18, 1893. Here was a new gospel of comradeship and loyalty that quickened every heart. No Dartmouth man can read these opening lines without exultation:

Again among the hills!
The shaggy hills!
The clear arousing air comes like a call
Of bugle notes across the pines, and thrills
My heart as if a hero had just spoken.
Again among the hills!
The jubilant, unbroken,
Long dreaming of the hills!
Far off, Ascutney smiles as one at peace;
And over all

The golden sunlight pours and fills
The hollow of the earth, like a god's joy.
Again among the hills!
The tranquil hills
That took me as a boy
And filled my spirit with the silences!

From a literary point of view "Men of Dartmouth" is unquestionably the finest college song in existence and has done much to interpret Dartmouth to the world. His "Dartmouth Ode" read at the one hundred twenty-fifth anniversary of the College, his poems read at the various banquets of the Dartmouth Alumni Associations have also interpreted the spirit of the College in beautiful and vigorous rhythms. Richard Hovey built up a little literature about Dartmouth such as no other college in America possesses. It is a heritage more precious than we now know. But some day when the things of the spirit are more real we shall see that Richard Hovey's call to manhood, to comradeship, to loyalty, to fellowship with all that makes Dartmouth the intellectual mother of us all, is part of the priceless spiritual endowment of the College.

The work by which Richard Hovey wished to be remembered was his retelling of the Arthurian legends, five volumes of the nine projected being completed at the time of his death. He will be remembered by many, however, for his three volumes of "Songs from Vagabondia" written in collaboration with Bliss Carman. Hovey regarded these lightly as the effervescence of his intimate friendship with Carman, Roberts, Meteyard, Kavanagh, and Parsons. It may well be that these lyrics of friendship will hold a larger audience than his more serious work, for the whole world loves a lover.

To Dartmouth men, Richard Hovey's college lyrics, particularly those associated with Dartmouth, will always have a peculiar and intimate appeal. Here he is writing of us in words and symbols that we can understand. He is saying the things we have striven to say, and failed.

EDWIN OSGOOD GROVER.

DARTMOUTH LYRICS

DARTMOUTH LYRICS

MEN OF DARTMOUTH

MEN of Dartmouth, give a rouse
For the college on the hill!
For the Lone Pine above her
And the loyal men who love her—
Give a rouse, give a rouse, with a will!
  For the sons of Dartmouth,
  The sturdy sons of Dartmouth—
  Though round the girdled earth they roam,
  Her spell on them remains;
  They have the still North in their hearts,
  The hill-winds in their veins,
  And the granite of New Hampshire
  In their muscles and their brains.

They were mighty men of old
That she nurtured at her side,
Till like Vikings they went forth
From the lone and silent North—
And they strove, and they wrought, and they died
  But—the sons of old Dartmouth,
  The laureled sons of Dartmouth—
  The Mother keeps them in her heart
  And guards their altar-flame;
  The still North remembers them,
  The hill-winds know their name,
  And the granite of New Hampshire
  Keeps the record of their fame.

Men of Dartmouth, set a watch
Lest the old traditions fail!
Stand as brother stands by brother!
Dare a deed for the old Mother!
Greet the world, from the hills, with a hail!
   For the sons of old Dartmouth,
   The loyal sons of Dartmouth—
   Around the world they keep for her
   Their old chivalric faith;
   They have the still North in their souls,
   The hill-winds in their breath;
   And the granite of New Hampshire
   Is made part of them till death.

COMRADES

Again among the hills!
The shaggy hills!
The clear arousing air comes like a call
Of bugle notes across the pines, and thrills
My heart as if a hero had just spoken.
Again among the hills!
The jubilant, unbroken,
Long dreaming of the hills!
Far off, Ascutney smiles as one at peace;
And over all
The golden sunlight pours, and fills
The hollow of the earth, like a god's joy.
Again among the hills!
The tranquil hills
That took me as a boy
And filled my spirit with the silences!

O indolent, far-reaching hills, that lie
Secure in your own strength, and take your ease
Like careless giants 'neath the summer sky—
What is it to you, O hills,
That anxious men should take thought for the
  morrow?
What has your might to do with thought or sorrow,
Or cark and cumber of conflicting wills?
Lone Pine, that thron'st thyself upon the height,
Aloof and kingly, overlooking all,
Yet uncompanioned, with the Day and Night
For pageant and the winds for festival!
I was thy minion once, and now renew
Mine ancient fealty—
To that which shaped me still remaining true,
And through allegiance only growing free.

So with no foreign or oblivious heart,
Dartmouth, I seek once more thy granite seat;

Nor only of thy hills I feel me part,
But each encounter of the village street,
The ball-players on the campus, and their shouting,
The runners lithe and fleet,
The noisy groups of idlers, and the songs,
The laughter and the flouting—
Spectacled comic unrelated beings
With book in hand,
Who 'mid all stir of life, all whirl of rhythms,
All strivings, lovings, kissings, dreamings, seeings,
Still live apart in some strange land
Of aorists and ohms and logarithms—
All these are mine; I greet them with a shout.
Whether they will or no, they greet me too.
Grave teachers and the students' jocund rout,
Class-room and tennis court, alike they knew
My step once, and they cannot shut me out.
But dearer than the silence of the hills,
And greater than the wisdom of the years,
Is man to man, indifferent of ills,
Triumphant over fears,
To meet the world with loyal hearts that need
No witness of their friendship but the deed.
Such comrades they, the gallant Musketeers,
Wrought by the master-workman of Romance,
Who foiled the crafty Cardinal and saved
A Queen, for episode—who braved
The utmost malice of mischance,
The utmost enmity of human foes,
But still rode on across the fields of France,
Reckless of knocks and blows,
Careless of sins or woes,
Incurious of each others' hearts, but sure
That each for each would vanquish or endure.

Praise be to you, O hills, that you can breathe
Into our souls the secret of your power!
He is no child of yours, he never knew

Your spirit—were he born beneath
Your highest crags—who bears not every hour
The might, the calm of you
About him, that sublime
Unconsciousness of all things great—
Built on himself to stand the shocks of Time,
And scarred, not shaken, by the bolts of Fate.
And praise to thee, my college, that the lore
Of ages may be pondered at thy feet!
That for thy sons each sage and seer of yore
His runes may still repeat!
Praise that thou givest to us understanding
To wring from the world's heart
New answers to new doubts—to make the landing
On shores that have no chart!
Praise for the glory of knowing,
And greater glory of the power to know!
Praise for the faith that doubts would overthrow,
And which through doubts to larger faith is
growing!
The sons of science are a wrangling throng,
Yet through their labor what the sons of song
Have wrought in clay, at last
In the bronze is cast,
And the wind and rain no more can work it wrong.

But more than strength and more than truth
Oh, praise the love of man and man!
Praise it for pledge of our eternal youth!
Praise it for pulse of that great gush that ran
Through all the worlds, when He
Who made them clapped His hands for glee,
And laughed Love down the cycle of the stars.
Praise all that plants it in the hearts of men,
All that protects it from the hoof that mars,
The weed that stifles; praise the rain
That rains upon it and the sun that shines,
Till it stretch skyward with its laden vines!

Praise then for thee, Psi Upsilon!
And never shame if it be said
Thou carest little for the head,
All for the heart; for this is thy desire.
Not for the social grace thou mayest impart,
Not for the love of letters or of art,
Albeit thou lovest them, burns thy sacred fire.
Not to add one more whip to those that drive
Men onward in the struggle to survive,
Not to spur weary brain and tired eyes on
To toil for prizes, not, Psi Upsilon,
To be an annex to collegiate chairs
Or make their lapses good!
Make thou no claim of use
For poor excuse
Why thou shouldst climb thy holier stairs
Towards ends by plodders dimly understood.
No, for the love of comrades only, thou!
The college is the head and thou the heart!
Keep thou thy nobler part,
And wear the Bacchic ivy on thy brow.

Comrades, pour the wine tonight,
For the parting is with dawn.
Oh, the clink of cups together,
With the daylight coming on!
Greet the morn
With a double horn,
When strong men drink together!

Comrades, gird your swords tonight,
For the battle is with dawn.
Oh, the clash of shields together,
With the triumph coming on!
Greet the foe
And lay him low,
When strong men fight together.

Comrades, watch the tides tonight,
For the sailing is with dawn.
Oh, to face the spray together,
With the tempest coming on!
Greet the sea
With a shout of glee,
When strong men roam together.

Comrades, give a cheer tonight,
For the dying is with dawn.
Oh, to meet the stars together,
With the silence coming on!
Greet the end
As a friend a friend,
When strong men die together.

—Hark, afar
The rising of the wind among the pines,
The runic wind, full of old legendries!
It talks to the ancient trees
Of sights and signs
And strange earth-creatures strong to make or mar—
Such tales as when the firelight flickered out
In the old days men heard and had no doubt.
O wind, what is your spell?
Borne on your cry, the ages slip away,
And lo, I too am of that elder day;
I crouch by the logs and hear
With credent ear
And simple marvel the far tales men tell.

There came three women to a youth, and one
Was brown and old, and like the bark of trees
Her wrinkled skin was rough to look upon;
And one was tall and stately, and her brow
Broad with large thought and many masteries,
Yet bent a little as who saith, "I trow;"
The third was like a breath of morning blown

Across the hills in May, so blithe, so fair,
With brave blue eyes, and on her yellow hair
A glory by the yellow sunlight thrown.

And the youth's heart flamed as a crackling fire,
For his eyes were full of his heart's desire.

And the old crone said to him, "Come,
For I will give thee Power."
And the tall dame said to him, "Come,
I will give thee Wisdom and Craft."
And the maid of the morning said to him, "Come,
And I will give thee Love."

And the youth was still as a burnt-out fire,
For he knew not which was his heart's desire.

Then spake the maid again:
"Oh, folly of men!
What thing is this whereat he starts and muses?
Not twice the Dames of Birth
Bring gifts for mirth.
Choose, if thou wilt; but he that chooses, loses."

. . . Night on the hills!
And the ancient stars emerge.
The silence of their mighty distances
Compels the world to peace. Now sinks the surge
Of life to a soft stir of mountain rills,
And over the swarm and urge
Of eager men sleep falls and darkling ease.

Night on the hills!
Dark mother-Night, draw near;
Lay hands on us and whisper words of cheer
So softly, oh, so softly! Now may we
Be each as one that leaves his midnight task
And throws his casement open; and the air

Comes up across the lowlands from the sea
And cools his temples, as a maid might ask
With shy caress what speech would never dare;
And he leans back to her demure desires,
And as a dream sees far below
The city with its lights aglow
And blesses in his heart his brothers there;
Then toward the eternal stars again aspires.

SPRING

I SAID in my heart, "I am sick of four walls and a ceiling.
I have need of the sky.
I have business with the grass.
I will up and get me away where the hawk is wheeling,
Lone and high,
And the slow clouds go by.
I will get me away to the waters that glass
The clouds as they pass,
To the waters that lie
Like the heart of a maiden aware of a doom drawing nigh
And dumb for sorcery of impending joy.
I will get me away to the woods.
Spring, like a huntsman's boy,
Halloos along the hillsides and unhoods
The falcon in my will.
The dogwood calls me, and the sudden thrill
That breaks in apple blooms down country roads
Plucks me by the sleeve and nudges me away.
The sap is in the boles today,
And in my veins a pulse that yearns and goads."

When I got to the woods, I found out
What the Spring was about,
With her gypsy ways,
And her heart ablaze,
Coming up from the south
With the wander-lure of witch songs in her mouth.
For the sky
Stirred and grew soft and swimming as a lover's eye
As she went by;
The air
Made love to all it touched, as if its care

Were all to spare;
The earth
Prickled with lust of birth;
The woodland streams
Babbled the incoherence of the thousand dreams
Wherewith the warm sun teems.
And out of the frieze
Of the chestnut trees
I heard
The sky and the fields and the thickets find voice
  in a bird.
The goldenwing—hark!
How he drives his song
Like a golden nail
Through the hush of the air!
I thrill to his cry in the leafage there;
I respond to the new life mounting under the bark.
I shall not be long
To follow
With eft and bulrush, bee and bud and swallow,
On the old trail.

When the wind comes up from Cuba
  And the birds are on the wing,
And our hearts are patting juba
  To the banjo of the spring,
    Then there's no wonder whether
    The boys will get together,
With a stein on the table and a cheer for everything.

For we're all frank-and-twenty
  When the spring is in the air,
And we've faith and hope a-plenty,
  And we've life and love to spare;
    And it's birds of a feather
    When we all get together,
With a stein on the table and a heart without a care.

For we know the world is glorious
And the goal a golden thing,
And that God is not censorious
When his children have their fling;
And life slips its tether
When the boys get together,
With a stein on the table in the fellowship of spring.

A road runs east and a road runs west
From the table where we sing;
And the lure of the one is a roving quest,
And the lure of the other is a lotus dream.
And the eastward road leads into the West
Of the lifelong chase of the vanishing gleam;
And the westward road leads into the East,
Where the spirit from striving is released,
Where the soul like a child in God's arms lies
And forgets the lure of the butterflies.
And West is East, if you follow the trail to the end;
And East is West, if you follow the trail to the end;
And the East and the West in the spring of the world shall blend
As a man and a woman that plight
Their troth in the warm spring night.
And the spring for the East is the sap in the heart of a tree;
And the spring for the West is the will in the wings of a bird;
But the spring for the East and the West alike shall be
An urge in their bones and an ache in their spirit, a word
That shall knit them in one for Time's foison, once they have heard.

Spring in the world!
And all things are made new!
There was never a mote that whirled

In the nebular morn,
There was never a brook that purled
When the hills were born,
There was never a leaf uncurled—
Not the first that grew—
Nor a bee-flight hurled,
Nor a bird-note skirled,
Nor a cloud-wisp swirled
In the depth of the blue,
More alive and afresh and impromptu, more thoughtless and certain and free,
More a-shout with the glee
Of the Unknown new-burst on the wonder, than here, than here,
In the re-wrought sphere
Of the new-born year—
Now, now,
When the greenlet sings on the red-bud bough
Where the blossoms are whispering "I and thou"—
"I and thou,"
And a lass at the turn looks after her lad with a dawn on her brow,
And the world is just made—now!

Spring in the heart!
With her pinks and pearls and yellows!
Spring, fellows,
And we too feel the little green leaves a-start
Across the bare-twigged winter of the mart.
The campus is reborn in us today;
The old grip stirs our hearts with new-old joy;
Again bursts bonds for madcap holiday
The eternal boy.
For we have not come here for long debate
Nor taking counsel for our household order,
Howe'er we make a feint of serious things—
For all the world as in affairs of state
A word goes out for war along the border

To further or defeat the loves of kings.
We put our house to rights from year to year,
But that is not the call that brings us here;
We have come here to be glad.

Give a rouse, then, in the Maytime
For a life that knows no fear!
Turn night-time into daytime
With the sunlight of good cheer!
For it's always fair weather
When good fellows get together
With a stein on the table and a good song ringing clear.

And do I not hear
The first low stirring of that greater spring
Thrill in the underworld of the cosmic year?
The wafture of scant violets presaging
The roses and the tasselled corn to be;
A yearning in the roots of grass and tree;
A swallow in the eaves;
The hint of coming leaves;
The signals of the summer coming up from Arcadie!

For surely in the blind deep-buried roots
Of all men's souls today
A secret quiver shoots.
An underground compulsion of new birth
Lays hold upon the dark core of our being,
And unborn blossoms urge their uncomprehended way
Toward the outer day.
Unconscious, dumb, unseeing,
The darkness in us is aware
Of something potent burning through the earth,
Of something vital in the procreant air.

Is it a spring, indeed?
Or do we stir and mutter in our dreams,

Only to sleep again?
What warrant have we that we give not heed
To the caprices of an idle brain
That in its slumber deems
The world of slumber real as it seems?
No—
Spring's not to be mistaken.
When her first far flute notes blow
Across the snow,
Bird, beast, and blossom know
That she is there.
The very bats awaken
That hang in clusters in Kentucky caves
All winter, breathless, motionless, asleep,
And feel no alteration of the air,
For all year long those vasty caverns keep,
Winter and summer, even temperature;
And yet when April whistles on the hill,
Somehow, far in those subterranean caves,
They know, they hear her, they obey her will,
And wake and circle through the vaulted aisles
To find her in the open where she smiles.

So we are somehow sure,
By this dumb turmoil in the soul of man,
Of an impending something. When the stress
Climbs to fruition, we can only guess
What many-seeded harvest we shall scan;
But from one impulse, like a northering sun,
The innumerable outburst is begun,
And in that common sunlight all men know
A common ecstasy
And feel themselves at one.
The comradeship of joy and mystery
Thrills us more vitally as we arouse,
And we shall find our new day intimate
Beyond the guess of any long ago.
Doubting or elate,

With agony or triumph on our brows,
We shall not fail to be
Better comrades than before;
For no new sense puts forth in us but we
Enter our fellows' lives thereby the more.

And three great spirits with the spirit of man
Go forth to do his bidding. One is free,
And one is shackled, and the third, unbound,
Halts yet a little with a broken chain
Of antique workmanship, not wholly loosed,
That dangles and impedes his forthright way.
Unfettered, swift, hawk-eyed, implacable,
The wonder-worker, Science, with his wand,
Subdues an alien world to man's desires.
And Art with wide imaginative wings
Stands by, alert for flight, to bear his lord
Into the strange heart of that alien world
Till he shall live in it as in himself
And know its longing as he knows his own.
Behind a little, where the shadows fall,
Lingers Religion with deep-brooding eyes,
Serene, impenetrable, transpicuous
As the all-clear and all-mysterious sky,
Biding her time to fuse into one act
Those other twain, man's right hand and his left.
For all the bonds shall be broken and rent in sunder,
And the soul of man go free,
Forth with those three,
Into the lands of wonder;
Like some undaunted youth,
Afield in quest of truth,
Rejoicing in the road he journeys on
As much as in the hope of journey done.
And the road runs east, and the road runs west,
That his vagrant feet explore;
And he knows no haste and he knows no rest,

And every mile has a stranger zest
Than the miles he trod before;
And his heart leaps high in the nascent year
When he sees the purple buds appear:
For he knows, though the great black frost may blight
The hope of May in a single night,
That the spring, though it shrink back under the bark,
But bides its time somewhere in the dark—
Though it come not now to its blossoming,
By the thrill in his heart he knows the spring;
And the promise it makes perchance too soon,
It shall keep with its roses yet in June;
For the ages fret not over a day,
And the greater tomorrow is on its way.

VAGABONDIA

OFF with the fetters
That chafe and restrain!
Off with the chain!
Here art and letters,
Music and wine,
And Myrtle and Wanda,
The winsome witches,
Blithely combine.
Here are true riches,
Here is Golconda,
Here are the Indies,
Here we are free—
Free as the wind is,
Free as the sea,
Free!

Houp-la!

What have we
To do with the way
Of the Pharisee?
We go or we stay
At our own sweet will;
We think as we say,
And we say or keep still
At our own sweet will,
At our own sweet will.

Here we are free
To be good or bad,
Sane or mad,
Merry or grim
As the mood may be—
Free as the whim
Of a spook on a spree—
Free to be oddities.

Not mere commodities,
Stupid and saleable,
Wholly available,
Ranged upon shelves;
Each with his puny form
In the same uniform,
Cramped and disabled;
We are not labelled,
We are ourselves.

Here is the real,
Here the ideal;
Laughable hardship
Met and forgot,
Glory of bardship—
World's bloom and world's blot;
The shock and the jostle,
The mock and the push,
But hearts like the throstle
A-joy in the bush;
Wits that would merrily
Laugh away wrong,
Throats that would verily
Melt Hell in song.

What though the dimes be
Elusive as rhymes be,
And Bessie, with finger
Uplifted, is warning
That breakfast next morning
(A subject she's scorning)
Is mighty uncertain!
What care we? Linger
A moment to kiss—
No time's amiss
To a vagabond's ardor—
Then finish the larder
And pull down the curtain.

Unless ere the kiss come,
Black Richard or Bliss come,
Or Tom with a flagon,
Or Karl with a jag on—
Then up and after
The joy of the night,
With the hounds of laughter
To follow the flight
Of the fox-foot hours
That double and run
Through brakes and bowers
Of folly and fun.

With the comrade heart
For a moment's play,
And the comrade heart
For a heavier day,
And the comrade heart
Forever and aye.

For the joy of wine
Is not for long;
And the joy of song
Is a dream of shine;
But the comrade heart
Shall outlast art,
And a woman's love
The fame thereof.
But wine for a sign
Of the love we bring!
And song for an oath
That Love is king!
And both, and both
For his worshipping!

Then up and away
Till the break of day,
With a heart that's merry,

And a Tom-and-Jerry,
And a derry-down-derry—
What's that you say,
You highly respectable
Buyers and sellers?
We should be decenter?
Not as we please inter
Custom, frugality,
Use and morality
In the delectable
Depths of wine-cellars?

Midnights of revel,
And noondays of song!
Is it so wrong?
Go to the Devil!

I tell you that we,
While you are smirking
And lying and shirking
Life's duty of duties,
Honest sincerity,
We are in verity
Free!
Free to rejoice
In blisses and beauties!
Free as the voice
Of the wind as it passes!
Free as the bird
In the weft of the grasses!
Free as the word
Of the sun to the sea—
Free!

HANOVER WINTER SONG

Ho, a song by the fire! Pass the pipes, pass the bowl;
Ho, a song by the fire! With a skoal, with a skoal!
Ho, a song by the fire! Pass the pipes, with a skoal!
For the wolf-wind is wailing at the doorways,
And the snow-drifts deep along the road,
And the ice-gnomes are marching from their Norways,
And the great white cold walks abroad.

Pile the logs on the fire! Fill the pipes, pass the bowl;
Pile the logs on the fire! With a skoal, with a skoal!
Pile the logs on the fire! Fill the pipes, with a skoal!
For the fire goblins flicker on the ceiling,
And the wine witch glitters in the glass,
And the smoke wraiths are drifting, curling, reeling,
And the sleigh-bells jingle as they pass.

Oh, a god in the fire! Pull the pipes, drain the bowl;
Oh, a god in the fire! With a skoal, with a skoal!
Oh, a god in the fire! Pull the pipes, with a skoal!
For the room has a spirit in the embers,
'Tis a god and our fathers knew his name,
And they worshiped him in long-forgot Decembers,
And their hearts leaped high with the flame.

Chorus

Zum, zum, zum, zum, zum, zum, zum,
But (For) (And) here by the fire we defy frost and storm,

Ha, ha! we are warm, And we have our hearts' desire.
For here's four good fellows, And the beechwood and the bellows,
And the cup is at the lip, in the pledge of fellowship.
Oh, here by the fire we defy frost and storm.
Ha, ha! we are warm, and we have our hearts' desire,
For here's four good fellows, and the beechwood and the bellows,
And the cup is at the lip, in the pledge of fellowship, of fellowship.

ELEAZAR WHEELOCK

OH, Eleazar Wheelock was a very pious man:
He went into the wilderness to teach the Indian,
With a *gradus ad Parnassum*, a Bible and a drum,
And five hundred gallons of New England rum.

The big chief who met him was the Sachem of the Wah-hoo-wah's
If he was not a big chief, there was never one you saw who was;
He had tobacco by the cord, ten squaws, and more to come,
But he never yet had tasted of New England rum.

Eleazar and the big chief harangued and gesticulated;
And they founded Dartmouth College and the big chief matriculated.
Eleazar was the faculty and the whole curriculum
Was five hundred gallons of New England rum.

Chorus

Fill the bowl! Fill the bowl!
And drink to Eleazar
And his primitive Alcazar,
Where he mixed drinks for the heathen
In the goodness of his soul.

DARTMOUTH ODE

I

Out of the hills came a voice to me,
Out of the pine woods a cry:

"Thou hast numbered and named us, O man. Hast thou *known* us at all?
Thou hast riven our rocks for their secrets, and measured our heights
As a hillock is measured. But are we revealed? Canst thou call
Ascutney thy fellow? Or is it thou Kearsage invites?
What speech have we given then, measurer—cleaver of stones?
For we talk to the day-star at dawning, the night-wind o' nights,
And our days are a tongue that thou hearest not, digger of bones!

"O you who would know us, come out from the roofs you have made,
And plunge in our waters and breathe the sharp joy of the air!
Let the hot sun beat down on your foreheads, lie prone in the shade,
With your hearts to the roots and the mosses, climb till you stare
From the summit that juts like an island up into the sky!
Watch the clouds pass by day, and by night let the power of Altair
And Arcturus and Vega be on you to lift you on high!

"For our heart is not down on the maps, nor our magic in books;

But the lover that seeks us shall find us, and keep in his heart
Every rune of our slow-heaving hillsides, the spaces and nooks
Of our woodlands, the sleep of our waters. His thoughts shall be part
Of our thoughts, and his ways shall be with us. His spirit shall flee
From the gluttons of fact. He shall dwell, as the hills dwell, apart.
He only that loves us and lives with us, knows what we be."

I hear you, O woods and hills!
I hearken, O wind of the North!

II

Daughter of the woods and hills, Dartmouth, my stern,
Rock-boned and wind-blown sibyl of the snows!
First in thy praise whom we can never praise
Enough, I lay my laurel in my turn
Before thee in thy uplands. No one goes
Forth from thy granite through the summer days.
And many a land of apple and of rose,
Keeping in his heart more faithfully than I
The love of thy grim hills and northern sky.

Mother of Webster! Mother of men! Being great,
Be greater; let the honor of thy past,
For which we sit in festival, elate,
Be but the portent of thy larger fate,
The adumbration of a deed more vast.
With eyes upon the future, thou and we
Shall better celebrate the past we praise,
And in the pledge of unaccomplished days
Find a new joy thrill through our pride in thee.

III

O Dartmouth, nurse of men, I see your games
To make men strong, your books to make them wise;
But there is other sight than that of eyes,
And other strength than that which strikes and maims.
What hast thou done to purge the passions pure,
To wake the myriad instincts that lie sleeping
Within us unaroused and undivined,
As forests in a hazel-nut endure;
To fashion finelier our joy and weeping,
Inspire us intuitions swift and sure,
And give us soul as manifold as mind;
To make us scholars in the lore of feeling,
And turn the world to beauty and revealing?

O justly proud of my first strenuous years!
Be not content that thou hast nurtured well
The hardy prowess of thy pioneers.
Among thy fellows bold, be thou the first,
Still guarding sacredly the antique well,
To seek our springs to quench the ages' thirst.
Take up the axe, O woodman of the soul,
And break new paths through tangled ignorance;
Dare the unknown, till on thy jubilant glance
The prairies of the spirit shall unroll.
For thou mayest teach us all that thou hast taught,
Nor slay the earlier instinct of the Faun,
Whose intimacy with earth and air withdrawn,
There rests but hearsay knowledge in our thought.
And thou mayest make us the familiars of
The woodlands of desire, the crags of fate,
The lakes of worship and the dells of love,
Even as the Faun is Nature's intimate.
For God lacks not his seers, and Art is strong,
And spirit unto spirit utters speech,
Nor is there any heaven beyond the reach
Of them that know the masteries of Song.

IV

Oh, the mind and its kingdom are goodly, and well for the brain
That has craft to discover and cunning to bind to its will
And wisdom to weigh at its worth all the wealth they contain.
But the heart has its empire as well, and he shall fare ill
Who has learned not the way of its meadows. His knowledge shall be
A bitter taste in his heart; he shall spit at his skill;
And the days of his life shall be sterile and salt as the sea.

Ay, save man's love be made greater, even knowledge shall wane,
And burn to the mere dry shrivelled mummy of thought,
As the sweet grass withers and dies if it gets not the rain.
But we—oh, what have we done that the heart should be taught?
We have given men brawn—without love 'tis the Brute come again;
We have given men brain—without love 'tis the Fiend. Is there aught
We have given to greaten the soul, we who dare to shape men?

Oh, train we the body for beauty, and train we the soul
Not only as mind but as man, not to know but to be!
Give us masters to fashion our hearts! Let the fool be a mole

And burrow his life out; the wise man shall be as a tree
That sends down his roots to the mole-world, but laughs in the air,
With his flowers, and his branches shall stretch to the sun to get free;
And the shepherds and husbandmen feed of the fruit he shall bear.

TO PROF. C. F. RICHARDSON

(For the dedication of a book)

SUCH as the seashore gathers from the sea—
Shells whose glad opal sunlight makes more glad,
And dead men's bones by bitter seaweed clad—
Teacher and friend, these songs I send to thee.
Gay things and ghastly mingled, seem to me
Here are alike; the merry and the sad,
The trivial and the tragic, good and bad,
For so I find the ways of life to be.
Evil and good are woven upon the loom
Of fate in such inextricable wise
That no man may be bold to judge and say,
"This thing is good, that evil," till the day
When God shall blazon on regenerate skies
The justice of His Pardon and His doom.

ONE LEAF MORE

Sir, I would do you honor in some way
  If my poor hand could lay a laurel more
On brows already thick with martial bay
  And ivy everygreen, the scholar's store,
And civic oak new-garlanded today
  To bind afresh where oft were bound before
Its fronds forensic and are bound for aye.

But you need not a poet's voice to tell
  The people who have honored you so long
Why they should love you whom they know so well.
  Still less does any here require my song
That he should praise you whom our hearts impel
  To hail with homage, heartfelt, deep, and strong,
To which my speech is but a tinkling bell.

Still let me praise you, though more fame accrue
  To me than you by praising. Praise is more
For him that gives than him to whom 'tis due.
  He that receives it has a bounteous store
And needs it not. Who gives, grows just and true
  By speaking justly. You are as before,
But we are better that we honor you.

THE LOVE OF A BOY — TODAY

Heigh-ho! my thoughts are far away;
For wine or books I have no care;
I like to think upon the way
She has of looking very fair.
  Oh, work is naught, and play is naught,
  And all the livelong day is naught;
  There's nothing much I care to learn
  But what her lovely lips have taught.

The campus cannot tempt me out,
The classics cannot keep me in;
The only place I care about
Is where perchance she may have been.
  Oh, work is naught, and play is naught,
  And all the livelong day is naught;
  There's nothing much I care to find
  Except the way she would be sought.

The train across the valley screams,
And like a hawk sweeps out of sight;
It bears me to her in my dreams
By day and night, by day and night.
  Oh, work is naught, and play is naught.
  And all the livelong day is naught;
  There's nothing much I care to be,
  If I be only in her thought.

A WINTER THOUGHT OF DARTMOUTH IN MANHATTAN

OLD Mother!
Mother off in the hills, by the banks of the beautiful river!
—River lacquered with pale green luminous ice,
Now, and the shouldered ridges ermined with flushed white snow—
Our thoughts go back to thee, Mother,
Straggle up the Connecticut, and by Bellows Falls and the Junction,
Find thee at last on thy hills, and embrace thy knees, old Mother.

We do not follow our thoughts upon that journey;
We have left thee, as men leave mothers,
Choosing and wedding their wives and cleaving thenceforth to them only.

Ah, she is stronger than thou, she who now holds us;
She that sits by the sea, new-crowned with a five-fold tiara;
She of the great twin harbors, our lady of rivers and islands;
Tower-topped Manhattan,
With feet reeded with the masts of the five great oceans
Flowering the flags of all nations, flaunting and furling—
City of ironways, city of ferries,
Sea-Queen and Earth-Queen!

Look, how the line of her roofs coming down from the north
Breaks into surf-leap of granite—jagged sierras—
Upheaval volcanic, lined sharp on the violet sky

Where the red moon, lop-sided, past the full,
Over their ridge swims in the tide of space,
And the harbor waves laugh softly, silently.

Look, how the overhead train at the Morningside curve
Loops like a sea-dragon its sinuous flight,
Loops in the night in and out, high up in the air,
Like a serpent of stars with the coil and undulant reach of the waves—

From under the Bridge at noon
See from the yonder shore how the great curves rise and converge,
Like the beams of the universe, like the masonry of the sky,
Like the arches set for the corners of the world,
The foundation-stone of the orbic spheres and spaces.

Is she not fair and terrible, O Mother—
City of Titan thews, deep-breasted, colossal-limbed,
Splendid with the spoil of nations, myriad-mooded Manhattan?
Behold we are hers—she has claimed us; and who has power to withstand her?

Nevertheless, old Mother, we do not forget thee.
Thine is the past!
Thine are the recollections, the love of the boyhood still in us,
As the sprout still lives in the bough and remembers March in midsummer.
Sword and engine and plowshare forget not the days
When the crude ore went to the smelting and the hammers rang on thy anvils.

This is a letter we send from ocean-dominioned Manhattan,
Bearing the love of a boy from the heart of a man,
Bearing the never-evading remembrance of thee and the hills and the river,
Thornton and Wentworth and Reed and the century-hollowed stairways of Dartmouth,
The old rooms where we laughed and strove and sang,
Where others now—hark, do I hear them?—
Sing in the winter night, while Orion rises and glistens.

THE OLD PINE

IT stood upon the hill like some old chief,
  And held communion with the cryptic wind,
Keeping like some dim unforgotten grief
  The memory of the tribesmen autumn-skinned,
Silent and slow as clouds, whose footing passed
  Down the remote trails of oblivion
Long since into the caverns of the past.
  Alone, aloof, strong fellow of the sun,
We chose it for our standard in its prime,
  Nor—though no longer grimly from its hill
It fronts the world, like Webster—wind nor time
  Has felled its austere ghost, we see it still,
In alien lands, resurgent and undying
Flag of our hearts, from sudden ramparts flying.

DAY AND NIGHT

FAIR college of the quiet inland lake
And beautiful fair name that like a bell
Rings out its clear sheer call of joy, Cornell!—
Its call of high undaunted dares that take
The hearts of men with fervours for thy sake,
And for thy sake with sudden hopes that swell,
Hail first to thee, with praise for thy bold youth,
Thy fearless challenge in the ranks of truth,
Thy forward footing into the unknown!
The new in knowledge that is old in being
Wrenched from the dark and morninged for our seeing—
This is the legend on thy banners blown.

Mightier the foes yet that are still to smite,
And fiercer yet the fields we still must fight,
But thou, a David of the sunrise cause,
In the first dawn of the defiant day,
Startled the mumbling hosts that bar the way—
Thou, a young Spartan of the days to be,
Made the vast hordes of Persian darkness pause
And bade our band think of Thermopylæ.

Day—yes, the day for thee! but all we men
Are twofold, having need of day and night.
Day for the mind, the ardour of the fight,
Night for the soul and silence. So again
To thee I turn, O one of many stars
That make the loyal heaven glorious,
But dear among the innumerable to us,
Psi Upsilon, and resting from the scars
Of day, the brunt of battle, lift thy song,
"Now for the joys of night!"—they sing it still
In the old chapters where we had our fill
Of fun and fellowship and frank good will,
I and my fellows, when we too were young.

"Soft as a dream of beauty"—hark, again!
Here's to his right good health who sang that strain!

Come with me into the night—
The intimate embracing night!
The night is still;
And we may walk from hill to hill
Silent, with but the murmur of our souls,
As through the woods the murmur of the night.
—Ah, take your heaven of undying light,
Of glare of gold and glint of aureoles!
I think God keeps for us somewhere
A place of cool dusks and caressing air,
Where all the greens and yellows dream of blue
And all the rainbow hints itself in hue
But never speaks outright—
Never unveils
The unmistakable red or violet,
But lets all color die to a perfume.

Is it the flapping of sails
And the lurch of a jibing boom
Where a boat comes round, below, on the lake, to set
Off shore again? How clear,
Like the league-distant hills that seem so near
In the thin air of Colorado, rise
The voices of the merry-making crew
Over the waters—songs of love that strew
The silence with the roses of surmise!

Hark!
There is no sound beneath the sky
But sails that flap and oars that feather
And the low water whispering by
In the June weather.
My love and I,
My love and I,
My love and I together!

The starlight lies upon the lake
Like dreams of vanished days and viewless
Earth never shall recall awake—
The dim lost Thules!
My love and I,
My love and I,
My love and I together!

The soft wind stirs among the firs,
The great stars wait above and seek not;
The night is full of ministers
For souls that speak not.
My love and I,
My love and I,
My love and I together!

I wonder whether you and I
Are real, love—I wonder whether!
I only know that, live or die,
We dream together.
My love and I,
My love and I,
My love and I together!

Far, so far—
The song dies on the waters like a star
That founders in the surges of the dawn.

Ah, the great Night!
The far phantasmal Night!
The delicate dim aisles and domes of dream!
Loosed from the mind, set free
From thought and memory,
The soul goes naked into the vast stream
Of musing spirit like a careless faun—
The soul lies naked to the summer night.

Night of the clasped hands of comrades! Night of the kiss

Of lovers trembling at love's mysteries!
Night of desire!
Night of the gaslight-necklaced city! Night
Of revel and laughter and delight!
Night of the starlit sea!
Night of the waves shot with strange witch-fire!
Night of sleep!
Night of dream!
Night of the lonely soul under the stars!

But ever the self put away
With the day,
And the soul soaring, glorying into the night!

Night!
The unmasked mysterious Night!
The infinite, unriddled beautiful Witch!
The Sibyl of the universal Doom!

This is the joy of man's spirit—
When peace falls,
Unknown, undivined, inexplicable,
Over the face of the world.

Oh, praise for the glory of battle—the Day and its strife!
And praise for the sweat and the struggle, the turmoil of life!
But the work is not wrought for the working, increase for increase;
We toil for the rest that comes after, we battle for peace.
Let us take up our work every man, meet our fate with a cheer—
But the best is the clasped hands of comrades, when nightfall is near,
The best is the rest and the friendship, the calm of the soul

When the stars are in heaven and the runner lies
down at the goal.

Let us take up our work as a nation, the work of
the day,
Clasp hands with our brothers of England—and
who shall say nay?
And who shall say nay to our navies—the ships
of us, sons of the sea?
And who shall say nay to our empires, to the law
that we set for the free?
But the best is the bond that's between us, the bond
of the brothers in blood,
The bond of the men who keep silence, as the night
when it falls on the flood,
As the night when it falls on the vastness, the splen-
dor and lone of the wave,
The bond of the English forever, the bond of the
free and the brave!

And at last when the bugles are silent or call but
to rouse
A cheer for the memory of crowned and victorious
brows,
When the drums beat no more to the battle, and
smitten in one,
The hearts of the nations uplift but one song to
the sun,
When, the law once made good for all peoples by
stress of the sword,
The spent world shall rest from its wrestling, clasp
hands in accord,
Then, best of all bests, in the silence that falls on
man's soul,
We shall feel we are comrades and brothers from
tropic to pole.
All men by the pledge of their manhood made one
in the will

To achieve for all men as their fellows each conquest o'er ill,
No glory or beauty or music or triumph or mirth,
If it be not made good for the least of the sons of the earth,
And the bonds of all bonds shall be manhood, the right of all rights
The right to the hearts of our fellows, to the love that requites
All the strain and the pain, and the fag, all the wrench of the day,
When the stars shine at last in the heavens and Night has its way.

OUR LIEGE LADY, DARTMOUTH

Up with the green! Comrades, our Queen
Over the hill-tops comes to convene
  Liege men all to her muster.
Easy her chain! Blithe be her reign,
Queened in our heart's love, never a strain
  Dimming her 'scutcheon's lustre!
Up with the green! God save our Queen!
Throned on the hills of her highland demesne,
Royal and beautiful, wise and serene,
      Our Liege Lady, Dartmouth!

Gallant and leal! Truer than steel!
Loyally gather about her and kneel
  Here at her flag's unfurling.
Welcome her near cheer upon cheer,
Shout till the hawk far above us may hear,
  Where the clouds in the sky are curling.
Starry her fame, Heaven-born dame!
Cannon and trumpet salute her high name!
Hear the ranks ring with the royal acclaim:
      Our Liege Lady, Dartmouth!

Laurel and vine, that shall we twine
Meet for her brow who sits under the pine
  Far from the mad town's jarring?
Gracious and fair, see in her hair
Jewels her noblest have brought her to wear,
  Won in the world's stern warring!
Stainless her throne! Royal and lone!
Born in the purple the sunsets have thrown
Over the mountains by God's grace her own,
      Our Liege Lady, Dartmouth!

Hail to the Queen! Look, where the green
Folds of her banners about her are seen,
  Flash of her knights cuirassed!

True-hearted throng, break into song!
  Shout as her ensign passes:
Up with the green! God save the Queen!
Throned on the hills of her highland demesne,
Royal and beautiful, wise and serene,
    Our Liege Lady, Dartmouth!

IN MEMORIAM
(*A. H. Quint*)

MOURN we who honored him but knew him not;
  Grieve ye who loved him, looking on his face;
  Be mindful, Dartmouth, of each strenuous trace
  That keeps his loyal record unforgot.
There is no faithlessness in grief, God wot;
  However high the hope or clear the gaze,
  There must be tears at every burial-place,
  Though through the tears the very sky be shot.
For death is like the passing of a star
  That melts into the splendor of the dawn.
  Were we beyond the air that blurs our sight
In the clear ether where the angels are,
  We should behold it still; but now, withdrawn
  In sunrise, lose it, looking on the light.

HERE'S A HEALTH TO THEE, ROBERTS!

HERE'S a health to thee, Roberts,
  And here's a health to me;
And here's to all the pretty girls
  From Denver to the sea!

Here's to mine and here's to thine!
  Now's the time to clink it!
Here's a flagon of old wine,
  And here are we to drink it.

Wine that maketh glad the heart
  Of the bully boy!
Here's the toast that we love most,
  "Love and song and joy."

Song that is the flower of love,
  And joy that is the fruit!
Here's the love of woman, lad,
  And here's our love to boot!

YOU REMIND ME, SWEETING

YOU remind me, sweeting,
  Of the glow,
Warm and pure and fleeting,
—Blush of apple-blossoms—
  On cloud-bosoms,
When the sun is low.

Like a golden apple,
  'Mid the far
Topmost leaves that dapple
Stretch of summer blue—
  There are you,
Sky-set like a star.

Fearful lest I bruise you,
  How should I
Dare to reach you, choose you,
Stain you with my touch?
  It is much
That you star the sky.

Why should I be climbing,
  So to seize
All that sets me rhyming—
In my hand enfold
  All that gold
Of Hesperides?

I would not enfold you,
  If I might.
I would just behold you,
Sigh and turn away,
  While the day
Darkens into night.

BARNEY McGEE

Barney McGee, there's no end of good luck in you,
Will-o'-the-wisp, with a flicker of Puck in you,
Wild as a bull-pup and all of his pluck in you—
Let a man tread on your coat and he'll see—
Eyes like the lakes of Killarney for clarity,
Nose that turns up without any vulgarity,
Smile like a cherub, and hair that is carroty—
Wow, you're a rarity, Barney McGee!
Mellow as Tarragon,
Prouder than Aragon—
Hardly a paragon,
You will agree—
Here's all that's fine to you!
Books and old wine to you!
Girls be divine to you,
Barney McGee!

Lucky the day when I met you unwittingly,
Dining where vagabonds came and went flittingly.
Here's some Barbera to drink it befittingly,
That day at Silvio's, Barney McGee!
Many's the time we have quaffed our Chianti there,
Listened to Silvio quoting us Dante there—
Once more to drink Nebiolo spumante there,
How we'd pitch Pommery into the sea!
There where the gang of us
Met ere Rome rang of us,
They had the hang of us
To a degree.
How they would trust to you!
That was but just to you.
Here's o'er their dust to you,
Barney McGee!

Barney McGee, when you're sober you scintillate,
But when you're in drink you're the pride of the
intellect;

Divil a one of us ever came in till late,
Once at the bar where you happened to be—
Every eye there like a spoke in you centering,
You with your eloquence, blarney and bantering—
All Vagabondia shouts at your entering,
King of the Tenderloin, Barney McGee!
There's no satiety
In your society
With the variety
Of your esprit.
Here's a long purse to you,
And a great thirst to you!
Fate be no worse to you,
Barney McGee!

Och, and the girls whose poor hearts you deraci-
nate,
Whirl and bewilder and flutter and fascinate!
Faith, it's so killing you are, you assassinate—
Murder's the word for you, Barney McGee!
Bold when they're sunny and smooth when they're
showery—
Oh, but the style of you, fluent and flowery!
Chesterfield's way, with a touch of the Bowery!
How would they silence you, Barney machree?
Naught can your gab allay,
Learned as Rabelais
(You in his abbey lay
Once on the spree.)
Here's to the smile of you,
(Oh, but the guile of you!)
And a long while of you,
Barney McGee!

Facile with phrases of length and Latinity,
Like *honorificabilitudinity*,
Where is the maid could resist your vicinity,
Wiled by the impudent grace of your plea?

Then your vivacity and pertinacity
Carry the day with the divil's audacity;
No mere veracity robs your sagacity
Of perspicacity, Barney McGee.
When all is new to them,
What will you do to them?
Will you be true to them?
Who shall decree?
Here's a fair strife to you!
Health and long life to you!
And a great wife to you,
Barney McGee!

Barney McGee, you're the pick of gentility;
Nothing can phase you, you've such a facility;
Nobody ever yet found your utility—
That is the charm of you, Barney McGee;
Under conditions that others would stammer in,
Still unperturbed as a cat or a Cameron,
Polished as somebody in the Decameron,
Putting the glamour on prince or Pawnee!
In your meanderin',
Love, and philanderin',
Calm as a mandarin
Sipping his tea!
Under the art of you,
Parcel and part of you,
Here's to the heart of you,
Barney McGee!

You who were ever alert to befriend a man,
You who were ever the first to defend a man,
You who had always the money to lend a man,
Down on his luck and hard up for a V!
Sure, you'll be playing a harp in beatitude
(And a quare sight you will be in that attitude)—
Some day, where gratitude seems but a platitude,
You'll find your latitude, Barney McGee.

That's not flim-flam at all,
Just the plain—Damn it all,
Have one with me!
Here's luck and more to you,
Friends by the score to you,
True to the core to you,
Barney McGee!

HUNTING SONG

Oh, who would stay indoor, indoor,
When the horn is on the hill? (*Bugle: Tarantara!*)
With the crisp air stinging, and the huntsmen singing,
And a ten-tined buck to kill!

Before the sun goes down, goes down,
We shall slay the buck of ten; (*Bugle: Tarantara!*)
And the priest shall say benison, and we shall ha'e venison,
When we come home again.

Let him that loves his ease, his ease,
Keep close and house him fair; (*Bugle: Tarantara!*)
He'll still be a stranger to the merry thrill of danger
And the joy of the open air.

But he that loves the hills, the hills,
Let him come out today! (*Bugle: Tarantara!*)
For the horses are neighing, and the hounds are baying,
And the hunt's up, and away!

WORLD AND POET

"SING for us, poet, for our hearts are broken!
  Sing us a song of happy, happy love!
Sing of the joy that words leave all unspoken!
  The lilt and laughter of life—Oh, sing thereof!
Oh, sing of life, for we are sick and dying!
  Oh, sing of love, for all our love is dead!
Oh, sing of laughter, for we know but sighing!
  Oh, sing of kissing, for we kill instead!"

How should he sing of happy love, I pray,
  Who drank Love's cup of anguish long ago?
How should he sing of life and joy and day,
  Who whispers death to end his night of woe?
And yet the poet took his lyre and sang
  Till all the dales with happy echoes rang.

MY LOVE'S WAITIN'

My love's waitin',
Waitin' by the river,
Waitin' till I come along!
Wait there, child; I'm comin'.

Jay-bird tol' me,
Tol' me in the mornin',
Tol' me she'd be there tonight.
Wait there, child; I'm comin'.

Whip-po'-will tol' me,
Tol' me in the evenin',
"Down by the bend where the cat-tails grow."
Wait there, child; I'm comin'.

ON THE HILL

Ah, God! here, here, Love bade me ope my still
  Shut heart-lips at his nod;
And here, in vain resistance to his will,
  I wrestled with the god.
What man can strive with Love? Is he not lord?
  Best conquest is to yield.
It was a victory to feel his sword
  Pierce through my idle shield.

I lay here at my queen's feet in the ashen,
  Wan June-light of the moon,
And sang to her the legend of my passion,
  A strange, forbidden tune.
The high gods cannot take away the glory
  Love gave me as I fell,
Nor dim the recollection of the story
  My lips took heart to tell.

Her eyes were filled with a divine compassion,
  Like starlight on the sea.
Sadly she spoke; and in a blind, dazed fashion
  I listened silently.
O stern denouncing pine! O cruel ledges!
  The grey years come and go.
Only for me no spring-time greens the hedges,
  No violets pierce the snow.

DEAD

Ah God! how strange the rattling in the street
  Comes to me where I lie and the hours pass.
I watch a beetle crawling up the sheet
That covers me, and curiously note
  The green and yellow back like mouldy brass;
And cannot even shudder at the thought
  How soon the loathsome thing will reach my face.

And by such things alone I measure out
  The slow drip of the minutes from Time's eaves.
For if I think of when I lived, I doubt
It was but yesterday I brushed the flowers;
  But when I think of what I am, thought leaves
The weak mind dizzy in a waste of hours.
  O God, how happy is the man that grieves!

Life? It was life to look upon her face,
  And it was life to weep when she was gone;
But this new horror!—In the market-place
A form, in all things like me as I moved
  Of old, is marked or hailed of many and one
That takes it for his friend that lived and loved—
  And I laugh voicelessly, a laugh of stone.

For here I lie and neither move nor feel,
  And watch that Other pacing up and down
The room, or pausing at his potter's wheel
To turn out cunning vessels from the clay,
  Vessels that he will hawk about the town,
And return to work another day
  Frowning, but I—I neither smile nor frown.

I see him take his coat down from the peg
  And put it on, and open the white door,
And brush some bit of cobwebs from his leg,
And look about the room before he goes;

And then the clock goes ticking as before,
And I am with him and know all he does,
And I am here and tell each clock-tick o'er.

And men are praising him for subtle skill;
And women love him—God alone knows why!
He can have all the world holds at his will—
But this, to be a living soul, and this
No man but I can give him; and I lie
And make no sign, and care not what he is,
And hardly know if this indeed be I.

Ah, if she came and bent above me here,
Who lie with straight bands bound about my chin!
Ah, if she came and stood beside this bier
With aureoles as of old upon her hair
To light the darkness of this burial bin!
Should I not rise again and breathe the air
And feel the veins warm that the blood beats in?

Or should I lie with sinews fixed, and shriek
As dead men shriek and make no sound? Should I
See her gray eyes look love and hear her speak,
And be all impotent to burst my shroud?
Will the dead never rise from where they lie?
Or will they never cease to think so loud?
Or is to know and not to be, to die?

WEDDED

BIRDS are singing in the closes—
  Singing for joy of June.
Scent of English violets
Mingles with the mignonette's;
And the garden's red with roses,
  When the glad brown thrushes croon—
Thrushes crooning in the closes
  All this rose-sweet June.

Rarer joy than yours has found me,
  Birds of the rose-sweet June!
Maidenhood with Maytime ended;
Love, the strong one, o'er me bended,
And with orange blossoms crowned me
  In the hot, sweet summer noon.
Rarer joy than yours has found me—
  Love's year has its June.

BOHEMIA

Us shall none bind;
Comrades, we're free,
Free as the wind,
Free as the sea—
Free!

O, why should we
Be the slaves of words?
Here we are free,
Free as the birds—
Free!

Free from the lies
We loath and despise,
Free to laugh,
Free to quaff
Rhine wine or lager beer—
Even whiskey
In our frisky
Moments here.

Here we are free;
Free to say
What we will;
Free to be sad,
Free to be gay;
Free to reveal
All we may be
Good or bad.

Here is the real,
Here the ideal,
Here the poor hardship
A week recalls not,
Here glory of hardship
That passes all thought.

True, sometimes troubles
May to us belong—
They are the bubbles
The stream does not heed 'em,
But flows along
In thunders of freedom
And tempest of song.

Laugh, you shallow
Worldling! Laugh,
You, too, callow
Beardless calf!
Laugh!

I tell you that we,
While you are smirking
And lying and shirking
Life's duty of duties,
Honest sincerity,
We are in verity
Free—

Free to rejoice
In blisses and beauties,
Free as the voice
Of the wind as it passes,
Free as the bird
In the weft of the grasses,
Free as the word
Of the sun and the sea—
Free!

SQUAB FLIGHTS

"Love is eternal," sang I long ago
  Of some light love that lasted for a day;
  But when the fleeting fancy passed away,
  And other loves, that following made as though
They were the very deathless, lost the glow
  Youth mimics the divine with, and grew gray,
  I said, "It is a dream: no love will stay."
  Angels have taught me wisdom. Now I know,
Though lesser loves and greater loves may cease,
  Love still endures, knocking at myriad gates
  That lead to God—stars, winds and waters, birds,
Beasts, flowers and men—speaking its sweetest words
  At woman's portal, till it finds its peace
  In the abyss where Godhead loves and waits.

A BALLADE OF MYSTERIES

Doctor, I pray you, do no more wrong
  To the drugged dog there in the horrid room.
Come, unmuzzle; disclose how the stars prolong
  Their lines of light through the infinite gloom,
  And how life grew in the young earth's womb.
Then I'll tell you how the bell's ding-dong
  Holds sweet talk with the birds i' the broom,
And the Poet's heart is astir with song.

Sage, who knowest to trace the throng
  Of world-thoughts further than bards presume—
Say how grows the weak babe wise and strong,
  And how is Thought born, and by whom
  Can the Fates be lured from the pitiless Loom,
And what is Right, and what is Wrong,
  Then I'll tell you why the breakers boom
And the Poet's heart is astir with song.

Priest, tell me now, ere the even song,
  How God lay hid in the Virgin's womb,
Who filleth the depth and height of the long
  Sky-reaches, and how bread should become
  His Flesh that rose from the Sacred Tomb.
Then I'll tell you how the clouds give tongue
  To God's message, the dream of the grand sweet doom,
And the Poet's heart is astir with song.

Envoi

Princess, say how the heart makes room
  For love in the halls where the statesmen throng,
Then I'll tell you why the roses bloom,
  And the Poet's heart is astir with song.

AT THE CLUB

(Rondel)

WHEN a pretty maiden passes
  By the window down the street,
  Cards and billiards lose their sweet;
Conversation on old brasses
Languishes; up go the glasses—
  "Nice complexion!" "Dainty feet!"
When a pretty maiden passes
  By the window down the street.

Smith forgets the "toiling masses,"
  Robinson the fall in wheat;
  All the club is indiscreet.
Ah! the wisest men are asses
When a pretty maiden passes.

WINTER BEAUTY

MID-WEEK of midwinter! Daybreak! It is snowing,
And I look out on my garden from my room,
Where a sixmonth since my roses were a-blowing—
Red and white and tea roses all in bloom.
Now the snow is falling, falling, still, relentless;
Everywhere the eye turns, only flakes of snow—
Ghosts of summer's rose leaves, colorless and scentless,
Come to haunt the gardens where they used to grow.

Ah! the ice-death that has slain the laughing river!
Ah! the memories of meadowland and mere!
Of the June-snow of pond-lilies lost forever,
And the roses that were blooming yester-year!
There is beauty in this cruel winter, even,
In this white world where the snowlight shimmereth;
But the beauty of the summer was of heaven,
And the beauty of the winter is of death.

VITA NUOVA

(Sonnetta doppa)

DANTE! when first I read the history,
  Enwrit herein by thee,
  Of all that infinite love that thou didst have
  For Bice from the day when thou didst see
  First her sweet symmetry
  And thy child heart was taken for her slave,
I was as one who sails across a sea,
  Elate of spirit and free
  As the glad gulls that laugh along the wave,
  And hears the sirens singing fitfully
  A mystic melody,
  Luring him to a melancholy grave.
With sweetest music, tender Florentine!
  Thou didst allure me through this little grove
  And in the midst thereof
  Showed me a place where cypress trees did twine
Their sombre ombrage; yet I saw above
  An opening in the trees where through did shine
  A ray of light divine,
  Quivering with pulses of eternal love.

KRONOS

As one of those huge monsters of the sky,
Fierce with the flame of fiery floating hair,
Falls from the zenith through the upper air,
Hurling the planets from their paths on high,
Jarring creation from its harmony,
Spreading on earth destruction and despair,
Terrifying men to the temples and vain prayer,
So from the summit of his majesty
He fails, and heaven is shaken as flame; Zeus reigns
Usurping; and no matter what is left—
How smooth or tangled grows his god-life's weft—
With how swift footing or how slow the years,
Speed on, for him forever there remains
A thunder and a chaos in the spheres.

A ROSE

Triolet

You thought I would not keep this rose,
  And yet I swore to kiss it nightly.
This only grieves me—to suppose
You thought I would not keep this rose.
There still the leaves lie, and it blows
  Here in my heart each day more brightly.
You thought I would not keep this rose?
  (And yet I swore to kiss it nightly.)

SONNETS — TO SWINBURNE

POET! thou art to me a faëry king
  Dwelling in some weird place of witchery,
  Some garden where unnumbered roses vie
  In color with the hollyhocks that spring
On every side in scarlet wantoning
  And lilies 'neath the gaudier herbage lie
  And violets unclose their leaves near by
  While stately sunflowers guard each opening.
And in that garden-realm magnificent
  I often see thee walking—stopping now
  To list to hollow murmurs, now to scent
Some flower's subtle perfume, wherein, pent,
  A rich, rare pleasance lies that none but thou
  And thy strange fellow-bard, the wind, can know.

Oft, too, I see thee on the rocky shore,
  Worshipping all the infinitely strong
  Grand godhead that to ocean doth belong,
  Or prostrate with uncovered head before
The sun, whom even Ocean doth adore,
  Who giveth speech to every poet's tongue,
  Who is the only king and god of song,
  From whom all bards receive their secret lore.
For thou art brother of the elements;
  There is a spirit of kinship that compels
  Your feet to stray in paths, where nothing dwells
Save the triune power that knows not death nor birth
  But sways all nature in omnipotence—
  Sea, wind and sun, the gods who rule the earth.

I, also standing where the white caps seem,
  In inextinguishable laughter on the shore,
  Forever tumbling and where, glancing o'er
  The sandy beach, the sun-god's arrows gleam,
Bright as the swords of Eden's cherubim,

Here, on this coast mind-seen of bards of your
Atlantis, the lost world now found once more,
This land whereof the Hellene did dream—
I cast this sea-shell into the great sea
And all the old Greek spirit in me prays
To great Poseidon, whom we both adore,
To cast it up upon the other shore,
Where it may meet thine Apollonian gaze
And murmur sweetlier, being seen of thee.

COLLEGE DAYS

For the Fly-Leaf of an Autograph Album

THESE college days of jollity and mirth—
  How pleasurable are they and how serene,
  Just tinged with sorrow enough to welcome in
  With heartier joy all wassail that gives birth
To bliss that lifts the spirit from the earth!
  Shall not this book and the signatures herein
  Of men whose friendship I am glad to win,
  Years hence recall this time that knows no dearth
Of ready jests and sunshine of sweet lays
  And vintages of Xeres and the Rhine?
  Ah! the remembrance of these happy days,
The music and the laughter and the wit,
  The cups that smile with glimmering of sweet wine—
Age shall grow mellow with the thought of it.

DANTE GABRIEL ROSSETTI

GONE art thou, then, O mystical musician!
  Pure-thoughted singer of these sinful years!
  No more shall dreams and doubts and hopes
    and fears
  Pass and repass before thy stricken vision;
No more from thine high sorrowing position
  Shall fall thy song-irradiated tears;
  Alas! no more against our listening years
  Shall new lays ring from thy lone lute elysian.
For unto thee at last has rest been given,
  Whether in sleep eternal by the shore
  Of Time's wide ocean or in song without
Or break or flaw, by the gold bar of that heaven
  From which the Blessed Damozel leaned out,
  Sighing for thee in the sad days of yore.

THE SOUTH

AH! where the hot wind, with sweet odors laden,
  Against the roses faintly beats his wings,
  Uttering mild melodious murmurings
  To the faint flowers and the fluttering gladen,
Whispering of some far, sunset-bowered Aidenn,
  And in an orange tree an oriole sings,
  Whereunder lies, dreaming of unknown things,
  With orange blossoms wreathed, a radiant
    maiden—
There is the poet's land; there would I lie
  Beneath the shadows of magnolia trees
  And let my eyes grow languid and my mouth
Glow with the kisses of the amorous breeze
  And breathe with every breath the luxury
  Of the hot-cheeked, sweet, heavy-lidded South.

LALAGE

My love is like the dawning
  And I am like the lark
That sings to greet her coming,
When 'neath a rosy awning
  In a golden cloud winged bark,
Upon a gittern strumming,
  She drives away the dark.

To the melody she strummeth
  Upon that gittern gay,
When o'er the hills she cometh,
I sing a song of sadness,
Though the tune she plays is merry,
And my sadness and her gladness
Mingle, chording in a very
  Dulcet and harmonious way.

My love is like the lily
  And I am like the rose
And the garden that we grow in
Is odorous and stilly;
And she is white and chilly
But I am red and glowing
  As a fire amid the snows.

Yet her love, so chaste and chilly,
  And mine, so warm and glowing,
Blend quietly and stilly,
As the waters of a river
  With the waters of the sea;
Ah! with love of her I quiver
  And she trembles, loving me,
  In the garden that we grow in.

Lalage! Lalage!
  Like a snowdrop thou art chilly—

Yet, enfolden in my bosom,
Like a snowdrop meltest thou
In the summer of my kisses.
I am bird and thou art blossom
But we swing upon one bough.
Oh, the love of thee and me,
Pale and virgin lily!
There is nothing sweet as this is,
Lalage!

But the dawning dawns not ever
And the lark not always sings
And the flowers must sometime wither—
We only meet to sever,
From our joy our sorrow springs
And unhappiness is hither
Borne on pleasure's purple wings.

TRANSLATION FROM THE ANACREONTEA

WHAT shall I do to you? What shall I do to you,
    Twittering Swallow?
Shall I pluck your light wings, you pestering scold?
Or tear out your tongue, as did Tereus of old?
Say, why do you wake me ere day is begun,
From beautiful dreams of my beautiful one?
What shall I do to you? What shall I do to you,
    Twittering Swallow?

JOHN KEATS

If thou canst not from some superior sphere
Look down upon this world that gave thee birth
Or from some glad abode of stingless mirth
Bend hitherward thy godbright head to hear
Some rainbow-winged etherial messenger
Tell thee men worship now thy wondrous worth,
If thou art not, having passed away from earth,
If thou whose name all sons of song revere
Art nothing but the shadow of a name,
If through the whole allotted period
Of thy brief life thou were allowed to dwell
In endless bitter ignorance of thy fame,
Then must we yield it that there is no God
Or else that he is crueller than hell.

SONNET

WHEN we are dead I firmly do believe
We shall slip back into the primal sea
Of the universal life, that there shall be
No such false joys as on this earth deceive
—Nay, nor no truer ones—nor cause to grieve
Nor terror nor despite nor mockery
Nor love, life's strongest bitterest mystery
And while we still are struggling in the strife
Surely it is a gracious boon though small
That one brief sweet real joy at least there is,
To be about to die and know that all
The anguish and the agony of life
Will not last longer than a lover's kiss.

TO A FRIEND

ALL too grotesque our thoughts are sometimes. Odd,
That there will come a day when you and I
Shall not be you and I! that we shall lie—
We two—i' the damp earth-mould—above each clod
A drunken headstone in the neglected sod—
Thereon the phrase, "Hic Jacet," carved awry,
And then our virtues, Bah! and piety—
Perhaps some cheeky reference to God!
And haply after many a century
Some spectacled old man shall drive the birds
A moment from their song i' the lonely spot
And make a copy of the quaint old words—
They will then be quaint and old—and all for what?
To fill a gap in a genealogy.

PHILOSOPHY

I SOMETIMES long to throw my books away
And to forget the thoughts that make me sad—
The mighty musings that have ever clad
The minds of men in chill and sombre grey.
I sometimes long to laugh out and be gay
As some blithe, thoughtless, merry-hearted lad
Or wander in the forest and be glad
Without a memory of a heavier day;
Yet when I try to turn myself apart
From all the deeper mysteries of Life
In nature-love and hate of human strife,
Still the same thoughts throng through my throbbing brain
And I arise in heaviness of heart
And turn me to my studying again.

AN AUTOBIOGRAPHY

THE following autobiographical sketch is the only authoritative account of the life of Richard Hovey in existence, and it seems worth while to preserve it here in association with his distinctively Dartmouth verse.

It was prepared at the request of the editor of this volume while still an undergraduate and a part of its data was used in an article by him entitled "Dartmouth's Laureate" which appeared in the June, 1894, issue of the *Dartmouth Literary Monthly* of which he was then managing editor.

In justice to Mr. Hovey it should be stated that the sketch was not written for publication in its present form yet for historical reasons it is left as he wrote it.

Ancestry:

On my father's side, I am descended from Daniel Hovey who settled in Ipswich, Massachusetts, in 1637. It is a matter in which I have some pride that for eight generations all the Hoveys in the line by which I descend (from Daniel, the emigrant ancestor, to my brother), have been pioneers—each one pressing on to the settlement of a new country. My great-grandfather and his immediate relations, by blood and marriage (the Slafters, Smiths, etc.), were the original settlers of the country about Hanover (Hanover, Thetford, Norwich, etc.). The Hoveys are supposed to be of Dutch extraction. Antoon van Hove was a Dutch historian and Latin poet (b. 1505; d. 1568).

I am also descended on my father's side from the Arnolds, who claim descent from Cadwallader and the Welsh kings; and from Robert Cushman, the agent of the Puritan colony in Holland, who hired the *Mayflower* for their use, but sailed himself in the *Speedwell* which was obliged to put back, being unseaworthy. He came to Plymouth the next year, 1621, in the *Fortune*, and preached the first sermon ever delivered in New England which was printed. Also descended from his son, Elder Thomas Cushman, and Mary Allerton, his wife, both of whom came over in the *Mayflower*. Mary Allerton was the youngest person on the *Mayflower* and outlived all the other passengers on that famous ship. Her father was Lieutenant-Governor Isaac Allerton of Plymouth colony, also a Mayflower emigrant.

On my mother's side, I am descended from the Spoffords, who trace their lineage to Gamelbar de Spofford, whose father, Gamel (son of Orm), was treacherously murdered by Earl Testi before the Conquest.

Also from John Coggeshall, first Governor of Providence Plantations, who was descended from an old English family, after whom the town of Coggeshall in England was named, and whose ancestry reaches back to the twelfth century.

Also from Peter Folger of Nantucket, the grandfather of Benjamin Franklin. The Folgers are supposed to be of Flemish origin.

Parents:

My father, Major-General Charles Edward Hovey, was born in Thetford, Vermont, 1827. Graduated at Dartmouth in the class of 1852. Studied law, but became more interested in educational work. Went to Illinois and founded the Illinois State Normal University of which he was the first president. Resigned the presidency of this institution at the outbreak of the Civil War to enlist as a private soldier in the Thirty-Third Illinois Volunteers. Was elected Colonel of that regiment by the votes of its members and commissioned Colonel by Governor Yates in 1861. Promoted to be Brigadier-General in 1862. Brevetted Major-General in 1865, "for gallant and meritorious conduct in battle, particularly at Arkansas Post, January 11, 1863." Has been since the war a practising lawyer in Washington, D. C. (General Hovey died in Washington in 1899.)

My mother, Harriette Farnham (Spofford) Hovey, was born in Nantucket, 1834—spent her childhood in North Andover, Massachusetts. Has been prominently interested in pedagogy always.

Life:

I was born in Normal, Illinois, May 4, 1864. Passed my childhood chiefly in Washington, spending the summers at North Andover, at old Spofford place there, owned at that time by my grandfather. Entered Dartmouth in the class of 1885, with which I graduated. Took the prize for dramatic speaking in 1884 and again in 1885. Was one of the commencement speakers, and a Phi Beta Kappa man. Took final honors *cum laude* in English language and literature. Was a member of the Psi Upsilon fraternity, and its delegate to the convention of 1885 at Hartford. Was an editor of *The Dartmouth* in my freshman, sophomore and junior years; and managing editor of the '85 *Ægis*. I wrote the sophomore history of my class, under the title, "Hanover by Gaslight; or Ways That Are Dark."

I lived in four or five places while I was in College, but the room I look back upon as mine was the corner room nearest Thornton in the top story of Reed Hall. The first recognition of any possible merit in my verses, the first encouragement I received, was from Prof. C. F. Richardson, on the occasion of my printing in *The Dartmouth* some sonnets to Swinburne. For Professor Richardson's words at that time I have never ceased to be very grateful.

1885-86 was spent in Washington, studying drawing and painting in the Art Students' League of that city.

The summer of 1886 I studied Hebrew at Professor Harper's Summer School of Hebrew at Newton Centre, Massachusetts.

1886-87 I was a junior at the General Theological Seminary of the Episcopal Church at Chelsea Square, New York. I was at the same time an assistant of Father Brown at the Church of St. Mary the Virgin. In consequence of an "incompatibility of temper" between myself and the authorities of the seminary, I left that institution, by the advice of my bishop, at the end of the first year, to pursue my studies privately under the bishop's direction. Practical necessity compelled my attention in other directions and I gradually drifted out of the intention of becoming a priest, without exactly knowing how or when I did so.

The summer of 1887 I was again at Newton Centre. It was during this summer that I met Tom Buford Meteyard, the painter, and Bliss Carman, the poet, who became afterward my dearest friends and who are now both associated with me in the "Songs from Vagabondia."

In the fall of 1887 I lived in Boston and did some newspaper work. I also made my first appearance on the stage as a "super" in the production of "Julius Cæsar" by Booth and Barrett.

I returned to Washington in the following winter. The next spring, as I was coming away from a lecture on "Sappho" at the Columbian University, I heard someone shouting behind me, "Hi! Holloa, there!" and turning round, beheld Hon. Horatio King (Postmaster General under Buchanan) running after me and gesticulating in a manner quite incomprehensible to me, as I had not at that time the honor of his acquaintance, nor would I in any case have expected so dignified a person to condescend to pursue me in the streets. I stopped till he came up, when he said that I looked like Giotto's portrait of Dante, and that he wanted to meet me. I went back, met Mr. Davidson, and was engaged that day to lecture for him the next June at his Summer School of Philosophy at Farmington, Connecticut.

The lecture I gave was on "Goethe's Mephistopheles and That of Marlowe." At Farmington I met Mrs. Lanier, widow of the late Sidney Lanier, and she presented me before I left with a wreath of laurel which had been sent her from the South. This was the occasion of my writing "The Laurel," of which a limited edition was published the following year.

In January, 1889, I planned the "Launcelot and Guenevere" series, and began "The Quest of Merlin."

In the summer of 1889 I lectured again at the Farmington Summer School of Philosophy, this time on the "Relations Between Ethics and Æsthetics."

In the spring of 1890 I went on the stage, primarily to complete my education as a playwright. My first part was with Mary Shaw in "A Drop of Poison." I played "Counsellor Fabricius," a diplomat at the court of Berlin.

In 1891 I went to Europe and spent a year in England and France. The greater part of this time was spent among the impressionistes and symbolistes painters in France, etc.

On January 17, 1894, I was married to Mrs. Henriette Russell at the residence of Benjamin Tenney, 308 Marlboro Street, Boston. Tenney was an '83 man (Dartmouth) and married Alice Parker, daughter of Professor Parker. Our civil marriage was performed by Maxwell, '83, and the religious ceremony by Professor Parker.

My wife is the leading living representative of the philosophy and art teaching of François Delsarte. She studied with the younger Delsarte in Paris and was his assistant there.

HISTORICAL NOTES

Men of Dartmouth. Page 3.

This poem won a prize offered by the Dartmouth Lunch Club of Boston, and another prize of one hundred dollars offered in 1894 by Henry M. Baker, '63, of Bowe, N. H., for the best poem suitable for a Dartmouth song. It was first published in the *Dartmouth Literary Monthly* for June, 1894, accompanying an article entitled "Dartmouth's Laureate" by the editor of the present volume.

Another prize of one hundred dollars was then offered by Mr. Baker for the best musical setting for the poem. No acceptable setting was made until 1898, when the prize was awarded to Addison F. Andrews, '78, and the song first appeared in "Dartmouth Songs," compiled by the editor of this volume and musically edited by Mr. Andrews.

In 1908 another setting for the song was made by Harry R. Wellman and published in "Songs of Dartmouth," compiled by the editor of this volume and Mr. Wellman.

Comrades. Page 5.

This poem was read at the Sixtieth Annual Convention of the Psi Upsilon Fraternity at Dartmouth College, May 18, 1893. The poem was read by Hovey at an open meeting held in the old gymnasium. The lyric, "Comrades Pour the Wine Tonight," was set to music and published in the first edition of "Dartmouth Songs."

Spring. Page 12.

Read by Hovey at the Sixty-third Annual Convention of the Psi Upsilon Fraternity at the University of Michigan, May 7, 1896.

Some years ago, in a contest conducted by *Collier's Weekly*, the "Stein Song" was voted the most popular college song in America. It was set to music by Frederick Field Bullard and first published in the first edition of "Dartmouth Songs" in 1898.

Vagabondia. Page 20.

This poem was read at the banquet of the Boston Dartmouth Alumni Association in 1889 and occasioned wide comment in the newspapers. The original draft of this poem was written while Hovey was an undergraduate and appeared in *The Dartmouth* for March 14, 1884 under the title "Bohemia." (See page 61.)

Hanover Winter Song. Page 24.

This song was written at the suggestion of the editor of the present volume for the first edition of "Dartmouth Songs," published by him in 1898. As Hovey's profession was that of letters, he was paid for this song, also for "Eleazar Wheelock" and other songs written for the editor. Hovey arranged for the musical setting by the noted composer, Frederick Field Bullard.

Eleazar Wheelock. Page 26.

This poem was written for the editor of the present volume for the first edition of "Dartmouth Songs" and was set to music by Miss Marie Wurm, an English composer and friend of Hovey's.

Dartmouth Ode. Page 27.

This Ode was read by Hovey at the One Hundred Twenty-fifth Anniversary of the founding of Dartmouth College, celebrated in Hanover in 1894.

To Prof. C. F. Richardson. Page 32.

Professor Richardson, familiarly known as "Clothespins," was for twenty-nine years the head of the Department of English at Dartmouth. Hovey often acknowledged his indebtedness to him as a great teacher, a wise critic and a loyal friend. This sonnet was written for the dedication of a book.

One Leaf More. Page 33.

When Joseph R. Hawley was reëlected to the United States Senate in 1893, Hovey read this poem at a dinner given in Hawley's honor by the Psi Upsilon Association of Washington, D. C.

The Love of a Boy—Today. Page 34.

This poem was written in 1897 for the editor of the present volume for use in the first edition of "Dartmouth Songs." No satisfactory musical setting was secured and it was not included.

A Winter Thought of Dartmouth in Manhattan. Page 35.

This was written for the annual banquet of the Dartmouth Alumni Association in New York City, in 1898 and read by Hovey.

The Old Pine. Page 38.

This sonnet was written in 1895 and was published in the "Songs of the Hill Winds," edited by Kendall Banning and Moses Bradstreet Perkins in 1901.

Day and Night. Page 39.

This poem was read by Hovey at the Sixty-sixth Annual Convention of the Psi Upsilon Fraternity at Cornell University, Ann Arbor, Mich., in 1899.

Our Liege Lady, Dartmouth. Page 45.

This poem was written in 1891 but was not published until it was included in the first edition of

"Dartmouth Songs." The musical setting was by Miss Marie Wurm, an English composer and friend of Hovey's.

In Memoriam. Page 47.

This sonnet was written in memory of A. H. Quint of the class of 1846.

Here's a Health to Thee, Roberts. Page 48.

This toast is to Charles G. D. Roberts who, with Bliss Carman the Canadian poet, and Tom B. Meteyard the painter, spent so many happy summers at the Nova Scotia home of Thomas William Parsons, the Dante scholar, for whom Hovey wrote his famous eulogy entitled "Seaward." It was set to music by Frederick Field Bullard and published in 1897 in sheet music form and included in the first edition of "Dartmouth Songs" in 1898.

You Remind Me, Sweeting. Page 49.

This first appeared as a lyric in the "Marriage of Guenevere." It was set to music by C. D. Milliken, '87, and included in the first edition of "Dartmouth Songs."

Barney McGee. Page 50.

This rollicking poem, which is a *tour de force* in rhyming, first appeared in "More Songs from Vagabondia." It was set to music by Frederick Field Bullard and was published in the first edition of "Dartmouth Songs," compiled by the editor of the present volume.

Hunting Song. Page 54

This lyric was written for "King Arthur," one of Hovey's dramas of the "Launcelot and Guenevere" series. It was first published in *The Chap-Book* for October, 1894, and included in the first edition of "Dartmouth Songs" with a musical setting by Arthur F. M. Custance.

World and Poet. Page 55.

During the spring of 1894 the writer, who was then an undergraduate and managing editor of the *Dartmouth Literary Monthly*, arranged for an Alumni number. This sonnet was Hovey's contribution. It was later included in "Songs of the Hill Winds," a collection of Dartmouth poems edited by Kendall Banning and Moses Bradstreet Perkins in 1901.

My Love's Waitin'. Page 56.

This lyric in dialect appeared as an interlude in a long poem "June Night in Washington" included in "More Songs from Vagabondia." The editor of this volume arranged with Ethelbert Nevin, the famous composer, to set it to music and it was included in the first edition of "Dartmouth Songs."

On the Hill. Page 57.

This poem was published in the *Dartmouth Literary Monthly* for February, 1887 and later included in "Dartmouth Lyrics," edited by B. A. Smalley, '94, and issued in 1893.

Dead. Page 58.

Hovey contributed this poem to the January, 1893, issue of the *Dartmouth Literary Monthly.*

Wedded. Page 60.

This was first published in the *Dartmouth Literary Monthly* for June, 1888.

Bohemia. Page 61.

This poem was written during Hovey's junior year and first appeared in *The Dartmouth* for March 14, 1884. It is interesting as being the basis for the longer poem, "Vagabondia" (see page 20), read by Hovey at the Dartmouth Alumni banquet in Boston some years later.

Squab Flights. Page 63.

This sonnet was contributed to the *Dartmouth Literary Monthly* for April, 1888.

A Ballade of Mysteries. Page 64.

Hovey contributed this ballade to the *Dartmouth Literary Monthly* for October, 1887.

At the Club. Page 65.

This rondel first appeared in the *Dartmouth Literary Monthly* for December, 1887.

Winter Beauty. Page 66.

This sonnet first appeared in the *Dartmouth Literary Monthly* for February, 1887.

Vita Nuova. Page 67.

This poem was first published in the February 20, 1885 issue of *The Dartmouth.*

Kronos. Page 68.

This was written during Hovey's senior year and contributed to *The Dartmouth* for April 17, 1885.

A Rose. Page 69.

First published in the *Dartmouth Literary Monthly* for April, 1888.

Sonnets to Swinburne. Page 70.

These sonnets appeared in *The Dartmouth* for March 2, 1883, Hovey's sophomore year, and were praised by Prof. C. F. Richardson which, according to Hovey, was the first literary recognition he ever received.

College Days. Page 72.

This sonnet was written during Hovey's junior year and contributed to *The Dartmouth* for March 30, 1883.

Dante Gabriel Rossetti. Page 73.
From *The Dartmouth* of March 30, 1883.

The South. Page 74.
From *The Dartmouth* of April 20, 1883.

Lalage. Page 75.
From *The Dartmouth* of May 18, 1883.

Translation from the Anacreontea. Page 77.
From *The Dartmouth* of November 9, 1883.

John Keats. Page 78.
A sonnet from *The Dartmouth* of April 18, 1884

Sonnet. Page 79.
From *The Dartmouth* of October 31, 1884.

To a Friend. Page 80.
From *The Dartmouth* of April 17, 1885.

Philosophy. Page 81.
From *The Dartmouth* of April 17, 1885.

www.ingramcontent.com/pod-product-compliance
Lightning Source LLC
LaVergne TN
LVHW021428110826
845150LV00007B/2138

* 9 7 8 1 4 2 5 5 0 6 7 2 8 *